Awareness Is the Key:

Bettering Relationships Between Parents and Teens

MARY KERBACHER

September, 2014

Print information available on the last page

Rev. date: 04/20/2016

To order additional copies of this book, contact:
Xlibris
1-888-795-4274
www.Xlibris.com
Orders@Xlibris.com

A booklet of assistance for the parent and the teenager

Do they really know what they are doing?

How do they see themselves?

Drug and alcohol problems?

How can you help?

TABLE OF CONTENTS

The Purpose and Benefit of this Booklet

The purpose of this booklet is to gain awareness for the parent or guardian and the adolescent-teenager. In hopes that they may build better relationships through improving their communications; as they develop a better understanding of the problems they face today. Read on for awareness in how you can help yourself as well as one another.

Introduction

The teenage years are the time in one's life that promotes the sense of personal identity. This specific period of late childhood is characterized by normative upheaval and turmoil. Erikson (1956) named this conflict, "identity versus identity diffusion." Piaget (1969) insists in his study of cognition that this particular age has the highest level of intellectual development. This period is when the young person makes a final emotional separation from his or her parents and says good-bye to childhood. This is one's most difficult years for the normal teen, add trauma and this difficulty goes to a whole other level.

If you do not know where the difficulty lies, you cannot fix it.

Let's find it.

Parent's Awareness

Our culture persists that teenagers are frequently typecast as brooding idealists or impulsive delinquents and inherent in both roles is alienated from the adult community. Here are some things you can do to improve your relationship with your teen.

1. The biggest complaint of a teenager is that they feel their parents do not listen to them and what they say is not important. The teen will shut down and not talk even if something is bothering them. First of all, kids talk a different language and parents find it hard to have empathy. You want to look at them, acknowledge them, and give them an empathic response even if it feels weird. Always agree with their feelings and always use "I" statements. It works.

2. Does your teen cooperate and does your punishment fail?
First of all, do not approach them while you are angry. It is best to describe the problem, express your feelings strongly without attacking their character and state your expectations. Then show your teen how to make amends. Give them a choice of following the right thing or not, take action of what the consequences are and problem-solve. See what can be worked out that both of you agree upon.

3. If your child experienced any kind of trauma or abuse what to do?

Traumatic events overwhelm the ordinary human adaptions to life and they consist of: threats to one's life, bodily integrity or a close encounter with violence or death. They lose the sense of a safe base within oneself in relationship to others. It is not a good place for them to be in. The teen needs immediate treatment. First of all, do not blame them and stress to them how much you love them. Most importantly, tell them this is not their fault. Seek long-term treatment for they need rehabilitation of a weakened condition of self; not suppression of symptoms. The teen needs your empathy, greater cohesion and social competence to help them back to a progressive line of development. One of the most important things you can do is show quality parenting; a healthy, supportive and wholesome atmosphere, be trustworthy, honorable and heroic this can do wonders for the traumatized youth. The nature of a parent/child relationship is of greater significant than the overwhelming events. Always put the love and resilience of the teen before the tragedy.

4. How to help the problem child/disrespectful child?

Sometimes a teen will act out due to confusion over the parent's behavior. Sometimes we do not realize how our behaviors affect our children. First, we need to see if our behavior has been appropriate. Our children need consequences for their negative behaviors. Most importantly, if the child does not exhibit empathy, the best thing you can do is allow the child to see other's sufferings.

You can prepare a plan where they are involved in activities where they can help someone else. Examples are: read stories to children in the hospital, visit the elderly in a nursing home or spend time with underprivileged children. You may even get them a "Big Sister or Big Brother" from the court system.

5. How to build success in your teen?

You want to give your teen a realistic self-image, so you want to praise them correctly and healthy. The child may doubt the praise, have immediate denial, forced to look at weaknesses, be experienced in manipulation or feel uncomfortable. You want to stay away from words such as great, brilliant, wonderful and beautiful. Find a word that will tell your teen something good about him/herself that he/she may not have known before. This will give him/her a new snap-shot of him/herself. Every time you use this technique it will give your teen something to put into his/her emotional bank; can't be taken away but sure can cash it in when he/she needs it. These moments when their best is confirmed becomes lifelong touchtones which he or she can return to in times of doubt or discouragement. There is no doubt your teen will be more aware and appreciate one's strength. There is no value judgment more important to man than the estimate he passes on himself. The other thing to do is instead of evaluating—describe. Describe what you see such as "I see a nice clean bedroom." Describe what you feel "It is a pleasure to walk into this room and it smells fresh." Sum up your teen's praiseworthy behavior with a word or very few words "you took your time, that was considerate and that's what I call splendid." You want to avoid praise hints of past weaknesses, excessive enthusiasm and make sure your praise fits your teens level/age.

6. Helpful hints:

Before giving a teen a choice, make sure it is acceptable to you.

Allow your teen respect for positive or negative feelings.

Speak calm and appropriate to your teen for they learn through example.

Do not put your teen down.

Whenever they ask a question do not ever blow up.

The chief complaints from every teen that I have interviewed are: the teen does not feel their parents listen to them, their feelings do not matter and they do not feel respected.

Teen's Awareness

You probably talk to your friends far more than your parents and that is okay but; most of you do want a parent's help, advice and support. You can have a great relationship with your parents even though you want to find your own path and make your own choices.

Communicating with your parents or other adults can be stressful because it seems difficult or intimidating.

Here are some things that may help you:

1. Practice talking with your parents about everyday things; the more you do, the easier it gets. Plus, this will help you when you need to discuss something more important or serious.

If your relationship is strained, try talking about such things as; what do you think of the weather we've been having or ask how your brother did on his spelling test? Small talk with your parents every day will help keep your relationship strong or get stronger.

Find something each day to talk about; it does not have to be a lot but something. This will help keep the lines of communication open for you and you will be more comfortable.

2. How to talk about something difficult:

Know what you want from the conversation with your parents. Do you want advice, just listen or do you want something?

Although you are nervous, you want to recognize your feelings. It is natural to be nervous; adults are. For instance; you might say something like "Mom, I need to talk to you but I am embarrassed."

You always want to pick a good time to talk. Ask them if it is a good time to talk or plan a time to talk with them.

There are things you can do to help you communicate with your parents so they will take you seriously. Be honest, direct and clear so they can understand. Try to understand their point of view and try not to argue.

3. If you cannot talk to your parents, seek out another adult that you can trust. Seek out a relative, teacher or someone you know will listen, understand and believe in you.

4. Look at your failures as lessons. They are tools you will use to help someone else in the future. They are your experiences that no one can take from you.

We do not learn from doing things right; we learn from making mistakes.

Always consult an adult when you do have a failure for it is always good to talk to someone who has been there before.
Thomas Edison's teachers said he was too stupid to learn anything. He did not give up. It took him 1400 failures before he succeeded.

5. How to build your self-esteem?

We all have a mental picture of who we are, what we look like, how smart we are and what our weaknesses are. We start to develop this at a very young age. This is called our self-image. Our self-image is based on interactions we have with others and our life experiences.

Self-esteem is how much we feel loved, valued, accepted and how well we are thought of by others. It is how much we value, love and accept ourselves. How others see or treat us and how we see ourselves has a big impact on self-esteem.

There are times in our lives when our self-esteem can be damaged. This happens when someone important to us puts us down constantly. We also can put ourselves down by being too critical of ourselves.

Here are some things that can improve your self-esteem:

Try to stop thinking negative thoughts about yourself. When you are too critical of yourself, counter it by saying something positive about yourself.

Aim for accomplishments instead of perfection. Do things you are good at and do not put unrealistic expectations on yourself.

View your mistakes as learning experiences. We learn from making mistakes not from doing things right.

Know the things you can change and the things you cannot change.

Set goals, make lists and mark them off as you complete them.

Try new things.

Do things for other people, help them participate in something or just volunteer your time. When you feel like you are making a difference, that is a huge ego booster.

Parenting Styles

Child-rearing styles are different types of parenting behaviors toward many different types of situations. Our goal is to create an acceptable atmosphere of child-rearing. The type of parenting approach I used was the authoritative parenting style. Studies revealed that this style is the most successful approach. This style came natural to me. I believe in keeping balance and use things in moderation.

The authoritative parent style is accepting, involved, uses adaptive control techniques as well as appropriate autonomy granting. An authoritative parent is warm, loving, attentive, has empathy and a relationship with their child that is enjoyed and emotionally fulfilling. This parent is geared toward keeping a relationship with their child, so the child would come to them about anything confusing or conflicting in opposition to anyone else. They trust their parents. The authoritative parent also possesses competence, self-control and task persistence that allows for their child to make decisions as their child is ready to do so.

There are also three other parenting styles: the authoritarian; who can be cold at times, rejecting, demands using force and rarely listens to one's child. The second is the permissive; who is warm but inattentive, makes no demands and allows the child to do whatever the child wants. The third is the uninvolved parent; who is detached and expects nothing and gives nothing. This later parenting style is the most damaging to a child and in every aspect.

The advice I would give to any parent or child development professional is children need to trust someone. They need love and acceptance. I would recommend to search the definition of the authoritative parenting style and mimic those behaviors of that parenting style. If you do not feel them at the time, keep mimicking them and you will. Children need to feel wanted. They want you to be fair and honest. There is never a reason to put a child down. They are in the learning process.

Children want discipline even though they say different; this builds integrity in a child. We must give respect to our children to teach respect to our children!

AWARENESS IS THE KEY: BETTERING RELATIONSHIPS BETWEEN PARENTS AND TEENS

Drug and Alcohol Awareness

Drug and alcohol abuse can lead to addiction. It is a huge problem for our society today. There are not only parents that deal with their children using drugs but children dealing with their parents using drugs. Awareness is the key!

Let's take a look at the definition of addiction: obsessions with compulsions. I will break that down: obsessions are anything that keeps our mind occupied; we cannot stop thinking about it. "I want it so bad!" "How can I get it?"

The compulsion is the act of doing it no matter the consequences!

Please, help me !

Addiction is cunning, baffling and POWERFUL!

How do I know if I am ADDICTED?

If you cannot control your use, if you cannot stop using and if you use until you black out; chances are you need help!

There are different ways in which one becomes addicted; some people are addicted from the very first use, some keep using until they build tolerance and have to use more to get the same effect, some cross the line and some people use because they have so much pain that they just do not want to feel it. They use to cover the pain or problem.

Signs and symptoms of different drug use:

Cocaine: fast pulse, dilated pupils, anxious, talk a lot and cannot stay focused on anything too long.

Opiates: extremely good mood, scratching, pinned pupils, heart rated slow, talk a lot and can appear to be very active.

Alcohol: you can usually smell it on so the breathe, can appear with unsteady gait, slurred speech and can talk a lot.

Pot: you can smell it, pupils dilated, can appear lazy or unmotivated and can procrastinate.

What leads to addiction?

Not dealing with problems, peer pressure, having pain that will not go away, and continued desire to escape from reality.

How to prevent addiction?

Education---knowing what you are up against, dealing with your problems, avoiding peer pressure, talking to someone when things are bothering you and avoiding people, places and things that lead to using.

How to treat addiction?

Detoxification and drug rehabilitation, avoiding people, places and things that are associated with your using, support groups---AA-Alcoholic Anonymous, NA-Narcotic Anonymous, education about your disease, getting a sponsor, applying the "12 STEPS" of recovery to your life, and getting a "Higher Power" in your life.

Note: addiction is no joke; addiction will take your life. Most people want to believe it is not happening to them and denial is the very thing in addiction that takes your life. Denying there is a problem has a very high price. Denying that there is a problem of addiction has taken too many lives. JUST SAY NO! Awareness that there is a problem is the key and you are worth saving. Do not let anyone tell you any different. Accept it and get help!

The Alcoholic Anonymous "Big Book" quotes, "Acceptance is the answer to all my problems today. When I am disturbed, it is because I will not accept a person, place or situation as the way it is supposed to be and until I accept that person, place or situation as the way it is supposed to be; I can find no serenity for nothing absolutely nothing happens in God's world by mistake." "I must keep my mind on my acceptance and off my expectations for my serenity is DIRECTLY proportioned to my level of acceptance!"

If you feel you have a problem please call the AA/NA hotlines they can be located in all phones books, computers and smartphones…..just put AA or NA Hotlines in your search engine.

Resources for Parents and Teens

West Branch Drug and Alcohol Abuse Commission:
570-323-8543.

PATH PA--Treatment & Healing: Troubled Youths
570-321-7860.

White Deer Run
1-800-255-2335

Diakon Family Life Services:
570-322-7873.

Books and Online Resources:

"How to Talk So Kids Will Listen" author—Adele Faber & Elaine Mazlish.
(Best Seller—"Parenting Bible")

"Alcoholics Anonymous" Alcoholics Anonymous World Services, Inc.

Parenting: Communication Tips for Parents:
www.apa.org/helpcenter/communication-...

Parenting-communication with teenagers:
mbetterhealth.vic.gov.au/.../Parenting_c...

References:

1. Berk, L., E. (2014). *Exploring Lifespan Development*. (3rd ed). Upper Saddle River, New Jersey: Pearson Education Inc

2. Faber, A., & Mazlish, E. (1999). *How to talk so kids will* listen.

3. New York, N.Y: HarperCollins Publishers Inc

4. Janis-Norton, N. (2013). Will you please listen to me?!

5. *Scholastic Parent & Child,* 20.742, 44, 46-47. Retrieved from http://search.proquest.com.library.capella.edu/docview/1367 933267?pq-origsite=summon

6. Judith, M. M. (2001). Psychological trauma in adolescence:

7. Familial disillusionment and loss of personal identity.

8. *American Journal of Psychoanalysis, 61*(1), 63-83.

9. Retrieved from http://search.proquest.com.library.capella.edu/docview/204617607?accountid=27965 Keating, T. (2009). *Divine therapy: addiction.* Brooklyn,

10. N.Y: Lantern Books Lundborg, P., & Lindgren, B. (2004). Do they know what they are doing? risk perceptions and smoking behavior among swedish teenagers. *Journal of Risk and Uncertainty, 28*(3), 261-286. Retrieved from http://search.proquest.com.library.capella.edu/docview/203535166?accountid=27965

Printed in the United States
By Bookmasters